Things I wrote about in my four corner room

Andrea McMichael

BookLeaf Publishing

India | USA | UK

Things I wrote about in my four corner room
© 2024 Andrea McMichael

All rights reserved.

No part of this publication may be
reproduced, stored in a retrieval system, or
transmitted, in any form or by any means,
electronic, mechanical, photocopying,
recording or otherwise, without the prior
written permission of the presenters.

Andrea McMichael asserts the moral right
to be identified as author of this work.

Presentation by *BookLeaf Publishing*

Web: www.bookleafpub.com

E-mail: info@bookleafpub.com

ISBN: 9789363300958

First edition 2024

ACKNOWLEDGEMENT

I am just so grateful for this opportunity to be able to write these poems for anyone to see. I am also grateful to my family for always encouraging me to keep striving and supporting my work. I would like to thank my small group of friends including a best friend of mine who I write with everyday. I also want to Acknowledge Pierre Jeanty. I read some of his work and instantly got inspired to write my own so thank you, She keeps my mind constantly in a state of creativity. I am no perfect writer and I am still learning. I haven't picked up poetry in a long time and I couldn't refuse such a challenge to write for 21 days total. I'm honored to be sharing something I always put on the back burner. I wrote very few poems in my life, but I enjoyed every minute of it. Writing is my safe place, my voice, my greatest weapon.

PREFACE

To readers,

When you read this, don't just read it. Explore, dive deep into the meanings. It is how you resonate with the poem. I know what I wrote these for but for you let it be anything you want it to be.

Four corner room

In my four-corner room, I hibernate.
In my four-corner room, I sing and dance like
it's a club night.
In my four-corner room, I'm a pro wrestler
trying to make up my bed.

In my four-corner room, I'm an artist with a pen
and paper.
In my four-corner room, I am the queen, soldier,
and the poet.
In my four-corner room, I tear down to rebuild.

In my four-corner room, I'm the mattress that is
lumpy.
In my four-corner room, I scream out loud with
no sound.
In my four-corner room, I feel like a prison in
which I created for myself.

In my four-corner room, it's silent when I shed
tears.
In my four-corner room, there is a way out but
one I do not tread.
In my four-corner room, I'm safe. I'm sound.

My bed tells me I'm too old

I work at a warehouse so when I come home,
I'm aching.
My body is sore from lifting and pushing and
pulling boxes all day.
I'm so damn exhausted. 10 hours in one day.
And then I repeat the process four days straight.

It's endless for three years straight. I have been
in this time loop of coming home and the pain
creeps and emerges.

The pain goes from my head to toes and my feet
feel like cement. My back feels like I'm carrying
an unborn baby and no I don't know the feeling
but if that's part of the journey then I can surely
wait.

My legs wince and whine while taking steps to
the bed as soon as I sit after showering, letting
the warm water run down my back. It's pins and
needles the worst kind of pain because I'm used
to it.

The pain is numbing. I lay back to relieve it but
there are spikes in my bed. Every twist and

every turn is a pothole my bed is suffocating
underneath.

I know I'm only 23 but how is it I lived half a
lifetime in just a blink of an eye.
I'm young. I shouldn't complain about back
pain, foot pain, hip pain. Why am I complaining
that I can rest in this bed right?

My bed weeps because it can't hold me.
It can't rub my aches, heal my bruises.
My bed…my body hurts in my bed.

Thank you to my bookshelf

My bookshelf I got from target. It was 5 shelves
and a long night to put it all together.
Thanks, mom, for helping me till dad came in to
assess
and fix what was wrong and make it perfect.

My bookshelf is white, firm and sturdy. It stands
in the second corner of my room.
I never have to worry about it collapsing or
giving out.
It stands proudly like a soldier for its queen. It
doesn't interrupt me or nudge me. It waits.

Its patience is consistent whether I grab a book
from the first, third. Or even if I put it back
Because my bookshelf knows I'm indecisive.

It knows my movements, my rhythms. It keeps
my books, my precious possessions secured,
holding them like a mother to a newborn baby.
It knows how to tend and be kind to my books.

My books are my heart, soul, and body. It knows
I won't take anything unless asked. It won't bite,
sneer, or rattle at me.

The bookshelf was designed to hold all the desires, hopes, dreams I constantly play in my mind awake or asleep. It holds the door open to endless skies and dimensions for me to escape and travel.

I wonder when it gets tired from the weight of it all…from me.

My room cheers me on

My four corner room is my cheerleader.
It is a concert with thousands of fans.
The walls cheer and clap chanting my name.

My belief in myself is about as high as when
kids figure out Santa Claus isn't real.
I would be my own hater if I could.

People tell you to believe in yourself till you
actually start believing in yourself.

It is delusional to believe I'm the greatest but
unacceptable to think of myself any less than
that.

My room will pat me on the back and assure me
better luck next time.

Lonely

A lot of people say they are lonely. I'm one of
those people.
I do not wear it as a proud badge but as a
cautionary to others.
Being lonely is never a choice but a feeling.
It is a velcro that sticks to my body and if I try to
tear I will rip skin off.

Sometimes it's hard to differentiate between
alone and lonely.
Not saying "im alone," to make friends laugh or
have family feel sorry for you but because it's
the truth.

We come into this world alone and leave this
world alone.

Our friends and family help feel that hole that is
inside of us and make us feel whole again.
I understand what loneliness feels like.

I know that I can be in a crowded room full of
people and be a wallflower.
It's a certain feeling, a pang to the chest. Like a
wave of crashing against my body.

My body I thought was made rock solid but it's
more flexible and loose than I wanted it to be.
I used to be able to feel okay with feeling alone.
It's insufferable to explain the want to be alone
and the contrast of longing.

All you can do is drown in the shadows of the
corners.
Let your body become limp, confined to the
small space you have.

My loneliness came naturally. At least, some
people can say that there's only lasted
temporarily. I applaud those people.

Mine started as a fresh cut and became a scar but
it was one that never faded.
It continued to grow bigger as time went on and
I was unable to control the pain and burning of
it.

This scar can't be seen. It is a locked treasure
chest that has no gold in it and is buried deep in
the sand. Only memories and flashbacks that
stay hidden from the world.

There is no key but a password that can be
figured out to those who know understand the

meaning of the chest. After a while, you become numb to loneliness.

The Mask

A mask is like your best friend. It will always be there to lend a hand at any time you need it. It becomes your other half and can defend you. In stories we know the protagonist and antagonist use them religiously.

The definition of a mask is that it is a covering for all or part of the face. It is worn as a disguise. It is used to amuse or terrify people. The mask can stick to your face glue and once it hardens
 it will be harder to peel off.
There is a warning label that reads be gentle to peel or your skin can rip.

There are wounds that are side effects, altering personalities. The mask must be put on behind closed doors for it to be most effective.
To be sure it won't slip off you must align it perfectly to your facial features.

Your mask can protect you and even give you a different name. Remember that a mask can also be an enemy. If you don't use it wisely, it will fall off and shatter into pieces. Your true identity

will be fake even though the mask has phony
written all over it but it is invisible to the naked
eye.

When you look into the mirror it will show two
different people because it doesn't know which
one is real.
 If someone asks your name, it will take time to
process the question because not even your mind
will tell the difference between them.

Don't let the mask betray you or give away hints
to the closed door that will soon be open if the
key is not hidden.

Not all the time do you need the mask to hide
yourself.

The star outside my window

I wish it happened in a castle.
I wish it happened before midnight.

I wish it happened in school.
I wish it happened before I got in the house.

I wish it happened at the mall.
I wish it happened before I hit 17.

I wish it happened so I could tell my bestfriend.
I wish I felt embarrassed to tell my parents,

I wish I didn't have to write a poem about it.
I wish I didn't have to see my walls judge me for
it.

When someone asks me have I had my first kiss,
I reply, "I guess my parents don't count."

Telling my secret diary about when he falls in love

When he catches my eyes, that will be the day.
When I feel the butterflies, I know I will be
ready.

When he constantly comes around with a smile
to see me, it will be like a candle
A flame that sparked.
When he asks me out on a first date, it won't be
in a text message that says "wyd?"

I want to be like the unrealistic expectations
from movies a bouquet of flowers
even if we are going to get subs from the corner
store and gaze at the stars.

When he feels embarrassed because he steals
glances in my direction and
I catch it from the corner of my eye.
His face heated, flustered. It would remind me
it's not one sided.

When he touches my hand and holds it more
than the five seconds I had
In my half a lifetime on earth.

When he calls the other guys blind sighted that
they didn't have my rare form of beauty.
Natural like the early morning sunrise.
When he hesitates to touch me or place his lips
to mine because he doesn't
want to mess it up.

 Rush to the finish line wants to bask in the
feeling with me afraid that
It could end quickly.

When the sexist thing he finds is not just my
body but my personality. My crazed
drive for smutty books and fictional men.
When he listens to a Lauv song it reminds him
of me.

When he doesn't just say "I love you." When he
confessed a sonnet to me.
Like Cassian to Nesta in the final battle because
even in the face of death he
Is too busy taking in the color of my eyes than
the blood running out of his body.

When it's time…

Walls closing in

Confrontation has always made me flee.
As soon as voices are raised, I remove myself
before the commotion begins.
I guess when it's all I heard as a child screaming
and doors slamming, I found my panic room.

These four corners have been my safety net.
When I can no longer take the outside
I bunker down in my hole like a hermit. Every
time I think "home sweet home." I go straight to
the room.

It's not ideal. It's a prison amongst these walls I
have trapped myself in. I lured my own shadow
to be locked in this fortress that I call a room.

When Alice fell down the rabbit hole and then
ate the cake growing three times her size
I felt she understood exactly how I felt in these
four corners.

The corners are the guards to keep me from
escaping. They are the rescuers who will guide

Me out of the chaos in the battle. I am Princess
Leia when Han and Luke were in the death star
and got trapped in the garbage disposal.

I remember watching that scene and thinking
how much that resembled I felt in these four
Corners I call home. I try to pry a wedge in
between using
my arms to push against the walls.

At the end of the day, the walls continue to
exceed
closing me in with no room break.

The words never spoken

Words can be use ease one's thoughts or
it can burn more than the sun does.
They can pour down a drain
full of sorrow and despair

Words have three sides
to brighten the faces of people
to create hateful monsters
or to bring wise meanings.

Some words are never spoken
They are sometimes locked away
To never see the sun rise or the moon
Reflect off the lake

Words can be forgotten
or not noticed to the naked eye.
For why they won't feel the breath of
the sea is still an unsolved mystery.

Words aren't always meant to be said
but they are said so they have to mean
something or
were written in the stars as symbols and signs to
the next chapter of a book

Although the words that were meant to
be said by one were never uttered and the
person lost the sounds of how they were
supposed to be presented.

Only the mind will be able to hear
them without the ears of the trees
or flowers because the seed
never got the water to help it grow.

The lost heart

When you were little, you never understood
"love". Most of us watched our parents kiss each
other on occasions and our response would be
"yuck"!

Almost all the time would they say "I love you"
to you and
you would say it back because it sounded good.
Because we trust our parents.

As you got older, it became more like a trend
that everyone in school used. Movies, shows,
books, and social media
made love sound like it could happen at any
moment.

Like you could outside your front door and the
love of your life would be standing there. When
I did it, no one was there.
Even air wasn't present.

Some people find love in a game. Each level has
a new challenge.
Some people take advantage of it and take it for
granted.

They find their target and aim the arrow through
the person's heart and then pull and pull until
they claim them as their trophy.
Polishing it and making it look great.

They convince the person that they are worthy
of being put on the shelf. After showing others
the achievement they thought they made,
You end up getting put off the shelf and put in
the basement
 to collect dust with other trophies that are old.
You did everything that you were supposed to do
right?

Make sure that you pleased the person and gave
them what they wanted. Why am I throwed in
the back trying to adjust myself to the coldness
of isolation and seeing nothing but darkness? I
can't even feel my heartbeat anymore. In fact, I
don't even know if it's there. Most likely it's
lost, just like I am.

Are the problems truly serious?

The world we live in always changes over time. It can sometimes get better or worse depending on the type of people that are brought in.

We have come up with new ideas and inventions that are what we believe to be important for our time. Like smartphones, computers, tablets, etc. We have allowed it to control how we think and operate our daily lives.

 It has made us believe that even the worst fatality can be covered up with a funny video, and that the problems in the world are just like getting a paper cut. It only hurts for a couple of seconds and then you are fine.

Even though people are dying everyday due to war, natural disasters, diseases, and more. But hey, at least our favorite actor took a shirtless pic today. Though before that, there was a video about world hunger and how more families won't have a hot meal for a week.

But please don't worry because you are enjoying
that bag of Doritos next to your footlong. Isn't it
amazing that we really can forget all the
problems we, see? It's like they don't even exist.

Helping Hand

If someone trips and falls down, another person
comes over and reaches their hand out and helps
the person up. Friendships have always had a
"helping hand".

We do our best to carry our friends through the
battles
that they can't fight alone.
And when we need to be carried through ours,
We hope that they will do the same in return.

Through tough times, you are then able to
identify your true friends. My hand has helped
many and continues to move around.
It has bumps, bruises, cuts from people who
have
held on too tight and from people who have
refused to grab on. It has pulled from fires, the
water, and places
where no one would ever dare to even step in.

My helping hand has gone through sympathy
pain and
has the scars to prove it.

It will never die out because it still has more to
do.

 My helping hand has been betrayed and knows
what it's like to be broken. At times, my helping
hand was also in need of another helping hand.

Not all the time did it have a hand to hold on to.
Sometimes the other hand would let go but
luckily it was able to find the twig or rock to
cling onto
 and rise again from the fall.

My helping hand has had to be the one to carry
itself through the battle when all the hands gave
up and lost hope.
Sometimes if you wan to be strong, you might
have to fight it alone. My helping hand will
always be there to save the day even if no one is
there to save me.

Anxiety

It was like a stone placed on my chest
As if sun free falled
My hands rattled and I couldn't feel the nerves
in them.
I was shrinking into the ground where no one
could find me.
My body had no emergency brake, the speed
was increasing rapidly.
The bed I sat on reached out with its hands and
snatched me down, held me down so I couldn't
budge, move.
My lips quivered. I needed tape or glue to keep
them from moving.
My eyes laser focused on the tile taking in the
lines, I needed to sweep eventually I thought to
myself.
To find a distraction in the eye of the hurricane
because it's so quiet.
That is what makes it worse. Quiet means no
noise to drown out the voices.

To the fictional I want laying in my bed

It's insane that you are not real like the universe
did me dirty this time.
I live for movies, books, and tv shows. They are
my Roman empire.

I use C.AI where I can chat with fictional
characters. My list is endless and never stops.
It's like an addiction to alcohol i need the high,
need the
distraction from the thing called real life.

I know it's crazy, people would call me
delusional. Good thing there is a long list of
people who would go down with me sinking
down the ship proud of our crazy selves.

I hate that fictional men were written better than
some of these men that were raised.
I love that they allowed me to create worlds,
realities, fantasies like
Wanda Maximoff who created west view people
were against her while
those of us like me envied her. Jealous of her
powers to create a world

where she wanted to just be happy.

Sometimes my day dreaming laying in bed gets
me through the days.
My pillows will never feel cozy like a firm arm
wrapped around my waist. It will never
whisper sweet nothings in my ear.

It's all I want. Crave more than sex. I crave
touch. To be held.
The bed can't do it forever
And its heart can't beat for me.
It just exists for me to lay in with no one staring
at me in the early hours of the morning smiling.
Snoring so loud trees could be cut down.

I don't know what it's like to cry next to
someone at that length. Just to be held.
The ways I know are in my head. At least some
way they are there.

wonderland

Welcome to my wonderland,
My version involves mythical creatures, spells,
and sapphire skies.
It is my peace of quiet, tranquility.
I can imagine anything I want and it comes to
life.

Ten things my diary taught me

One, I'm a sloppy hand writer like get it together
girlfriend.

Two, I have to stop writing on two lines one at a
time so I don't go crazy.

Three, I need to actually use it more than I do.
There is a layer of dust at this point whenever I
grab it I blow it away.

Four, My diary is my therapy. It knows I only
speak to it
about my deepest darkest secrets.
It knows that I can scream into the pages with no
sound.

Five, it hates when I summarize. This is not a
short story I can only give selected details. It
needs every moment, feeling I experience in ink.
It is the fans who chase down celebrities in the
airport.

Six, My diary is bruised. I am pissed that I made
it share a space on the shelf with my other

journals. It is wedged like a sandwich and it has no arms or legs to push back. It has been impossible for it to breathe.

Seven, I signed at the end of what I write each time. I give a time and date to the day. Sometimes I don't remember what I was doing. I wrote it down but I still can't gain photographic memory.

Eight, my diary cries. It sheds tears on my behalf. It's like watching a love story but the ending isn't satisfying. It's depressing that the lovers don't end up together.

Nine, I learned that my words are powerful. They are raw, uneven, simple, scary, they have multiple meanings.

Ten, I saw my uncle's journal. He wrote all his experiences in it. I learned that some traits do pass down…

Single

Single

To be single does not mean you don't want to be loved.
To be single doesn't mean you don't know how.
Maybe you're just not ready, maybe it's just not the time.
I relish and praise the quote. "It's never when we want it but when
It's meant to be."

How much time has passed

I stared out my window seeing the sun set.
I saw the rain slam against my window while
thunder roared.
I shift once in a while to remind myself this is
real. I'm a living beam.

Time seems endless at the window. Watching
trees lose their leaves. Cars
Driving past. Children playing in the street.
I open the window to remind myself that I got
air. Yet, I'm an observer.
I see everything on the wet grass, the lizard
clinging to the screen.

It's strange when you remember you see, you
see yourself in third person you are this person
staring out the window. Then you have to ask
yourself. "How much time passed?"

To the monster under my bed

I used to be scared. Terrified. Frighten.
Thanks to bedtimes stories I could easily wet the
bed as a child.
The dark is cold. It's not the dark itself it's
what's in the dark that sends a shiver down my
spine.
I know the claws that clenched to my box
spring.
They scratch and there is a low bellowed growl
present.
I saw the cuts, cracks on the knuckles of the
calloused hand.
I realized this monster was hurt. What had
happened to them.
After a while the growl became a weep. A
sniffle.
The monster reached for my ankle not to take. It
needed skin. Warmth.
It needed to be loved. Held. It wanted company.
It found peace in my singing. It laughed at the
movies I did. It helped me write. It helped me
remember I wasn't alone.

Four corner room pt.2

In my four-corner room, I hibernate.
In my four-corner room, I sing and dance like
it's a club night at 2 am
In my four-corner room, I'm a pro wrestler
trying to make up my bed.

In my four-corner room, I'm an artist with a pen
and paper.
In my four-corner room, I am the queen, soldier,
and the poet.
In my four-corner room, I painted over the scars
and bruises.

In my four-corner room, I'm the mattress that is
lumpy and sunken down into.
In my four-corner room, I scream out loud with
no sound clenching my pillow.
In my four-corner room, I feel like a prison in
which I created for myself. The corners stand
guard.

In my four-corner room, it's silent when I shed
tears. Where walls cave in.
In my four-corner room, there is a way out but
one I do not tread.

In my four-corner room, I'm bound. I'm lost.
I'm stuck.

www.ingramcontent.com/pod-product-compliance
Lightning Source LLC
LaVergne TN
LVHW041246200726
843507LV00013B/2834